MW01406919

This notebook belongs to

____

20092841R00060

Made in the USA
San Bernardino, CA
26 December 2018